Printed in the United States of America

First Printing, 2016

ISBN 978-1545515129

Createspace Self Publishing

www.Createspace.com

This book is dedicated to the loves of my life. My husband Anthony Ifill, for always believing in me and standing by my side even when times were tough. And for my daughter for being her sweet little self. Mommy loves you!

"Wake up honey its morning, and we have a big day ahead of us. Come on sleepy head, today we are going to the zoo. There are so many animals waiting to meet you." Chelsea sat straight up in the bed, eyes wide with excitement, for the zoo was her favorite place to go. She rubbed her eyes and stretched her hands high above her head as she took a deep breath.

Chelsea was so excited for today was her birthday. She was finally six years old, and she knew she was a big girl now. She gave her mom a big hug and then hopped out of her bed. "Happy Birthday darling," said her mom, kissing her on her forehead. "Let's see, what should you wear today?" Her mom asked as she made her way to the closet. Chelsea ran to the window to peek outside. The sun was shining so bright up in the sky; she also heard the birds singing in the trees next to her window. Then she saw Mr. Andrews, the next-door neighbor, watering his garden in his favorite shorts. Chelsea smiled knowing it has to be warm outside.

"How about this?" her mom asked holding up a blue sweater. "No mom,' Chelsea laughed. "Why not?" asked her mom, "because that's for when it's cold and it's not cold outside today." Her mom smiled and reached back into the closet, pulling out a red rain jacket and matching rain boots. "What about this?" her mom asked. Chelsea giggled "no mom" "why not?" her mom asked again. "Because that's for when it's raining and it's not raining," said Chelsea. Chelsea's mom went back into the closet one last time and pulled out a yellow sundress with purple flowers all over.

"Will this do?" her mom laughed. "Yes!" Chelsea said excited for she was hoping her mom would pick that dress. After they were dressed, they headed downstairs where her father was waiting. Chelsea felt so special that she imagined she was walking down a grand staircase. "There's my birthday girl," her father said picking her up and swinging her in his arms. "Are we ready for the zoo today?" He winked at her mom knowing the special surprise they had waiting for Chelsea at the zoo.

"So what can I get the birthday girl for breakfast?" her mom asked. "Pancakes!" Chelsea yelled still in her father's arms. Her mom made animal shaped pancakes for everyone. She even let Chelsea pour the mix into the animal shaped cookie cutters she had bought just for Chelsea's special day. Chelsea chose the lion, as that was her favorite animal. She liked the way the lion cubs played and how cute and cuddly they were. After breakfast, it was off to the zoo. Chelsea sat in her booster seat as her mom pulled her seatbelt on, "safety first" her mom smiled and then off they went.

There were so many cars as they arrived at the zoo. It was such a beautiful day that other families decided to come to the zoo too. Chelsea was so excited; she could not wait to see all the different animals. As they walked closer to the zoo, Chelsea saw a guard looking inside everyone's bags. He winked at Chelsea, and as she and her family walked past the guard, Chelsea heard him say, "Welcome to the zoo." There was a gate they had to pass through first; there was a picture of a bear on the left and monkey on the right. Chelsea liked monkeys; she thought they were silly.

As they entered the zoo, the first animal they came across was a red panda. "They come all the way from China," said her mom, "and they are called red pandas because of the red and white fur that cover their whole body even their feet. They are only 42 inches tall and weigh 7 to 14 pounds; that's how much you weighed when you were born, 7 pounds and 6 ounces to be exact." Her mom laughed as she pinched Chelsea on the cheek.

The next animal they came across was a Rhinoceros. "These Rhinos live in the forest of Southeast Asia, and they can weigh over four thousand pounds!" Chelsea's dad picked her up and placed her on his shoulders and pointed in their direction as he continued. "They are very big animals, and they have a horn on the tip of their snout right on top of their nose. Their skin is really thick and gray, and they love to eat all types of leaves, fruits, and vegetables." "Yuck!" Chelsea frowned, she didn't like vegetables.

Next, they saw another big animal called the African elephant. A man with a round brown hat told the crowd of people that the elephant could reach up to fifteen thousand pounds. It has a long trunk, which is also their nose that was almost as tall as the man. "They can smell things that are very far away, and they can even use their nose as a water hose to clean themselves because they love to play in the mud and can get really dirty." Chelsea pretended to be an elephant by putting her two arms together to make a trunk as she began moving them up and down making the sounds she heard the big African elephant make. Next, they walked in the reptile building that was in the middle of the zoo.

There were all types of snakes, lizards, frogs, crocodiles and alligators. "Chelsea did you know that reptiles are cold-blooded animals," her dad said, "kind of like your Uncle Ned" her mom smiled gently nudging her dad on the arm. Her mom continued saying "they are cold blooded not because their blood is cold but because their temperature changes around to match the temperature outside." They walked toward the crocodiles and alligators as her mom said "A lot of people think that a crocodile and an alligator are the same, but they each have their own special differences.

An alligator's snout is shaped more like a U shape, and a Crocodile's snout is more like a V shape. Crocodiles also like living in salt water like the ocean while alligators like living in freshwater like lakes." Chelsea didn't like the alligators and crocodiles because they looked scary, and so off they went to see more of the animals. 'Rumble'. Chelsea looked down at her tummy. "Uh oh, I think someone is hungry," her dad said. They headed off to a nearby food stand.

"I wonder what goodies we can pick up here. He ordered three peanut butter and jelly sandwiches, three bananas and three juice boxes. They found a picnic table to sit and eat their food. "How are you enjoying the zoo?" Chelsea's mom asked. "I am having so much fun I can't wait to start again." After they had finished eating, Chelsea's dad made sure everything was clean before they headed back to the animals. "Where to now?" he asked while lifting Chelsea up on his shoulders. "To the monkeys," she said as she pointed the way. Chelsea started laughing and clapping her hands as they approached the chimpanzees.

When her dad put her down, she started to act out what she saw one of the monkeys doing as he came up close to her. She started running around with her hands held up and making sounds like a monkey. "Honey did you know that the chimpanzees are the smartest mammals in the world, besides humans of course. They are so smart that they have used them in the space programs." "Wow!" Chelsea was so amazed that she started acting like she was in outer space. "Look daddy I'm a monkey out in space," she said as she pretended to float around him. "Sweetheart did you know that chimpanzees are not monkeys, but they are actually part of the ape family like Gorillas and Orangutans, and they love to eat leaves, berries, seeds and different types of flowers" her dad continued. "Flowers!" Chelsea asked surprisingly. "You're supposed to smell flowers not eat them." Chelsea walked over to a flower, bent down and took a big long sniff; "Just like that" she added.

The day was coming to an end as more and more people were leaving the zoo. Chelsea's dad looked at her and said: "Your mom and I have a wonderful surprise for you." "For me?" Chelsea asked. "That's right," answered her mom. "It's your birthday surprise." Chelsea tried to imagine what her surprise might be. She pictured herself sitting on top one of the elephants and parading through the zoo. Then she imagined that she was swinging with the monkeys on the vines, but she knew that her mom would never allow her. Chelsea continued to think really hard about what it could be when her father began to speak. "We're here," he said, they were standing in front of the lion's den. "WOW!" Chelsea shouted. She never imagined that she would be allowed to ride a lion through the zoo.

She began to jump up and down flapping her hands all around. "Am I going to ride on a lion?" she asked as she roared and shook her pretend mane. "No, you silly goose," her mom said, "It's too dangerous to ride on a real lion." Her dad looked at her and said, "I have a friend here at the zoo, and he has a very special surprise for you." They walked into the building right behind the Lions. "Hi Chelsea my name is Phillip, and I am friends with your mom and dad, they told me how much you loved lions." Chelsea started nodding her head up and down really fast. "I have some lion cubs that were found without their mommy, and they are still very small, so they still need milk. Would you like to feed them?" Again, Chelsea nodded her head up and down; she was so excited that she couldn't even talk. Chelsea and her parents followed Phillip as he led them to the lion cubs.

Phillip handed Chelsea the bottle as she began to feed one of the cubs. "Look mommy it's drinking" her mom and dad came and stood beside her, "We have one more surprise for you." Phillip looked at her and said "how would you like this to be your cub? You can name her, and can come back to the zoo any time you want to play with her." Chelsea was so happy, she dropped the bottle and gave everyone a great big hug. "This is the best birthday ever, thank you so much!"

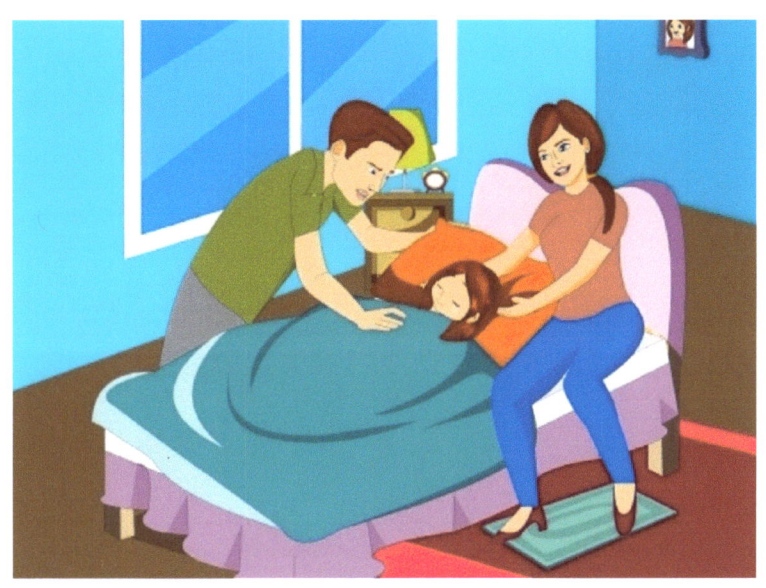

As they headed home from a wonderful day at the zoo, all Chelsea could think about was Layla, her new lion cub, until she fell asleep. As her mom and dad tucked her in she said, "This was the best day ever. Let's do it again tomorrow."

www.ingramcontent.com/pod-product-compliance
Lightning Source LLC
Chambersburg PA
CBHW040307010626
45792CB00025B/1452